Knights

© Aladdin Books Ltd 1996

Designed and produced by
Aladdin Books Ltd
28 Percy Street
London W1P 0LD

First published in the
United States in 1996 by
Copper Beech Books, an imprint of
The Millbrook Press
2 Old New Milford Road
Brookfield, Connecticut 06804

Design
David West Children's Book Design
Designer
Flick Killerby
Editor
Jim Pipe
Picture Research
Brooks Krikler Picture Research
Illustrators
McRae Books, Florence, Italy

Printed in Belgium

**Library of Congress Cataloging-in-
Publication Data**
Ross, Stewart.
Knights / by Stewart Ross: illustrated by McRae Books Agency.
p. cm. -- (Fact or fiction)
Includes index.
ISBN 0-7613-0453-3 (lib. bdg.). --
ISBN 0-7613-0468-1 (pbk.)
1. Knights and knighthood--History--
Juvenile literature.
I. McRae Books Agency. II. Title. III. Series: Ross, Stewart.
Fact or fiction.
CR4509.R58 1996   95-39831
940.1--dc20   CIP AC

FACT *or* FICTION:

Knights

Written by *Stewart Ross*
Illustrated by *McRae Books, Italy*

COPPER BEECH BOOKS

BROOKFIELD, CONNECTICUT

CONTENTS

INTRODUCTION

A cloud of dust on the horizon. Thundering hooves. A shout. The smell of sweat and leather. Enter horse and rider – the most powerful partnership in history.

Together they have conquered empires and built cities. They have traveled to the far corners of the world and spread news of their achievements. The dog may be our best friend, but the horse has truly been humankind's greatest ally.

Horse riding is woven into every culture. The mere mention of "horse" conjures up a host of images, and today we use words like "spur," "saddle," and "rein" without thinking of their original meaning.

Perhaps the most powerful image is the knight in shining armor. King Arthur or Sir Lancelot mounted on a beautiful white charger, so brave in battle yet the perfect gentlemen at court, were the epitome of chivalry.

But were the real knights really so courageous and so noble, and were the mounted Samurai bowmen really so invincible? In the American West, did the boys in blue of the U.S. cavalry always come over the crest of the hill in the nick of time? And was the Charge of the Light Brigade quite so magnificent?

Read on – and discover where fact ends and fiction begins!

IN DAYS OF OLD...

People have always been fascinated by the power, grace, and beauty of horses. Ancient pictures of wild horses adorn the walls of caves (*left*), yet for thousands of years horses were not helpers or friends but food, hunted for their meat and bones!

Then, perhaps over 15,000 years ago, nomadic tribes in Central Asia first learned to train horses to work for them. Once they were bred in captivity, the domestic horse and the wild horse grew apart. Before long, there was a wide variety of domestic breeds, including Arab horses, massive warhorses, and small ponies.

Horse races were featured in the first recorded Olympic Games (776 B.C.). But not until the development of the saddle and stirrup – again in central Asia – did the unique partnership of horse and human reach its height.

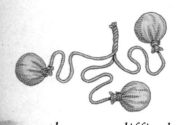

Dinnertime!
Stone Age humans (below) liked horses for a different reason than we do now – they ate them! Larger mammals, such as mammoths, were difficult and dangerous to hunt.

A lot easier to catch, the horse was also large enough to provide a good source of meat. Hunters used spears and bolas (above), a set of weights tied together and thrown to snare the horses' legs.

FROM FOOD TO FRIEND
As soon as humans learned to tame the horse, in about 12,000 B.C., they put the creature to use in war. Stone tablets show the Hittites training horses for sport and war in about 1400 B.C.

At first, single horses pulled battle wagons. Then came teams of horses, hauling larger chariots at higher speeds (page 8).

The Mongolian Wild Horse
The last remaining species of wild horse – Equus przewalskii – was found roaming the land of central Asia in about 1880. This horse is very similar to those hunted in the Stone Age.

KNIGHTS OF ANCIENT GREECE

Even before cavalry became an important battle-winner, the horse was a symbol of power and authority.

In ancient Athens, the population was divided between citizens, foreigners, and slaves (*right*). Citizens were divided into four ranks. Those in the second rank, originally wealthy enough to serve in the cavalry, were known as *hippes*, or horsemen.

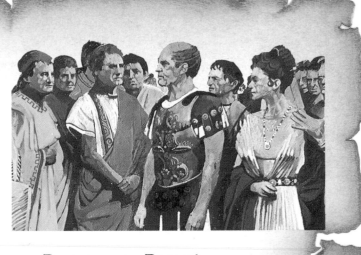

SHINY BOOTS AND BELTS!

For thousands of years, infantry and chariots remained the ultimate offensive weapons. But once a saddle and stirrups had turned the single horse into a stable fighting platform, expensive chariots fell into disuse and the infantry lost their power.

For the next 500 years, the powerful mounted knight was the ultimate military status symbol. Even today, the cavalry has a prominent position in any procession (*left*).

Most Excellent Wild Stallions (left)
The power of the wild horse – two stallions fight for leadership of the herd. Even horses born in captivity do not take kindly to being ridden. It must have taken a lot of skill and bravery for the first riders to mount wild horses.

"THE LADY OF SHALOTT." As you will discover, the heroic knight in armor is a powerful figure in European mythology. Nowhere is he more richly described than in this portrayal of Sir Lancelot in the poem *The Lady of Shalott* (shown right), by Alfred, Lord Tennyson (1809-1892):

All in the blue unclouded weather
Thick-jewell'd shone the saddle-leather,
The helmet and the helmet-feather
Burned like one burning flame together,
As he rode down to Camelot.

THE AGE OF THE CHARIOT

Over 5,000 years ago, by the banks of the mighty Euphrates River, an army of men stood ready to defend their land against the invader. Within minutes, however, they were crushed by a terrifying new weapon – battle carts pulled by wild donkeys!

The use of animals in war developed slowly from these humble beginnings. Within a thousand years horse-drawn chariots had appeared. The Indo-European tribes that swept into India and the Middle East from Asia in about 2000 B.C. used horse-drawn chariots and individual riders. Chariots were also used at Megiddo, the world's first recorded battle (in 1469 B.C.).

Horsemen rode with the chariots, but at this point were used for scouting and pursuing rather than launching an attack.

Saddle and Stirrup
First used in China in the 4th century A.D., the stirrup (top) reached Europe 400 years later. Saddles had arrived some 300 years earlier.

These inventions enabled riders to swing a sword without fear of falling off.

Chariots of Firepower
The lightweight Egyptian chariots were built as fast, mobile platforms for archers, who carried their arrows in quivers fixed to the side of the chariot (above).

At the battle of Kadesh in 1298 B.C., the chariots of Pharaoh Rameses II battled against heavily-armed Hittite chariots – the ancient version of a modern tank battle.

SWALLOWED IN THE RED SEA
The Bible says that Moses led the Israelites from Egypt across the Red Sea. When the Pharaoh (played by Yul Brynner, *left*) changed his mind and sent "all the chariots of Egypt" in pursuit, God closed the sea around them. This made a great scene in the epic film *The Ten Commandments*.

PARTHIANS AND NUBIANS

Archers from the Roman province of Parthia were famous for being able to shoot arrows backward while riding at full gallop.

But the most famous cavalry of the Roman era was used by Hannibal. His Nubian horsemen from North Africa destroyed the Roman legions at the Battles of Trebia (218 B.C.) and Cannae (216 B.C.).

Looks Aren't Everything

The Roman cavalry (right), *proud and well equipped, was in fact rarely used in attack. Without stirrups (see page 8), a galloping rider was likely to fall off when he swung his sword!*

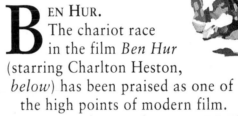

BEN HUR.
The chariot race in the film *Ben Hur* (starring Charlton Heston, *below*) has been praised as one of the high points of modern film.

But how realistic is it? Some of the "Roman" crowd can be spotted wearing modern wristwatches!

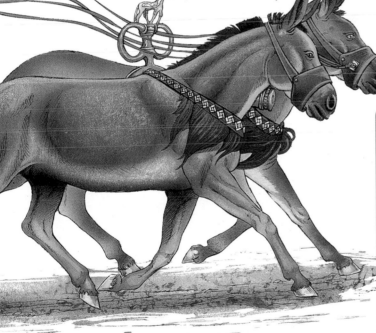

FOUR WHEELS ON MY WAGON

A war chariot of the Sumerian king Enannatum of Lagash (*above*).

Dating from about 2500 B.C., this solid-wheeled battle cart was one of the world's first horse-drawn vehicles. Unlike Egyptian chariots (page 9), these carried spear throwers.

A One Horse Town

Many great leaders had a favorite horse, but in 326 B.C. Alexander the Great (right) even founded a city, Bucephala (today's Jhelum in Pakistan), in honor of his horse Bucephalus.

BEASTS OF WAR AND MYTH

In the summer of 218 B.C. the Carthaginian general Hannibal led his army from its base camp in Spain and headed north. The Romans, thinking they were safe for that campaigning season, launched an attack across the Mediterranean on Hannibal's Spanish headquarters. It proved to be a disastrous mistake.

Hannibal took his 30,000 men, horses, and 37 elephants (see coin, *above*) across the Pyrenees and crushed the Gauls. In October, to everyone's amazement, he decided to take the Little St. Bernard Pass into Italy and launch a surprise attack on Rome itself. Fifteen days later he was in Italy, elephants and all!

Assisted by his war beasts, Hannibal won a series of brilliant victories. But in the end, deprived of support and reinforcements, he had to return home without capturing Rome.

STEEDS OF MYTH. The importance of horses to humans is reflected by their appearance in numerous legends. The mythical centaurs were half human, half horse inhabitants of the wooded foothills. They have been popular figures in folklore since the time of the ancient Greeks.

Pegasus (below) *was a mythical winged horse born out of the blood of the monstrous snake-haired Medusa.*

THE TROJAN HORSE
The world's most famous horse appears in a story from Homer's epic poem, *The Odyssey*. It was a huge model built by the Greeks for their enemies, the citizens of Troy. Odysseus and his Greek warriors hid inside the horse while the Greek army sailed away. Then the Trojans pulled the horse into the city.

Quick Victory
Once the horse was inside the walls, the Greeks opened the city gates. Troy fell soon afterward.

THE MYTHICAL UNICORN is a beautiful white horse with a single horn growing from its forehead (depicted *right* in the film *Legend*). Drinking from the horn was believed to give protection from illness.

Trunk Route (left)
The passes were blocked by snow when Hannibal led his war elephants through the Alps into Italy, fighting off local tribesmen as he went.

HANNIBAL'S HEAVIES
Once on the Italian plain, the elephants proved a useful shock tactic. But they needed to be cared for and were too slow and cumbersome to win a battle on their own.

THE SWEET SMELL OF SUCCESS!
In a story told by the Greek historian Herodotus, when Cyrus the Great of Persia's army met that of the Lydian king Croesus, the horrible smell of Cyrus' camels terrified the Lydian horses!

When their horses ran away, the Lydian cavalry were forced to jump down and fight on foot, and were soon beaten by Cyrus' troops.

Conquering Camels (right)
Camels were also used by the Arab soldiers of the 7th-8th centuries A.D. *They built a vast Muslim empire stretching from Spain to Persia.*

SADDLE AND SANDAL

The Age of Cavalry is said to begin with the Battle of Adrianople (A.D. 378), fought between the Romans and a mixed army of "barbarian" tribes from northern Europe, led by Fridigern. Fridigern's horsemen totally overwhelmed their Roman enemies and won the battle.

Infantry remained essential for carrying out sieges. But over the next 700 years the supremacy of cavalry became recognized all over Europe.

The Vikings and the Anglo-Saxons, who were fine foot soldiers, were among the last to accept the change. The weakness of their tactics was conclusively proved at Hastings in 1066 (*above left*).

THE LESSON OF SENLAC HILL

In 1066, King Edward of England died childless. Three men disputed the throne: Earl Harald of Norway, the English Harold Godwinsson, and Duke William of Normandy. The council accepted Godwinsson to take the crown, to become King Harold.

King Harold's foot soldiers resisted an invasion by Harald of Norway, then marched south to face Duke William. The two armies met near Hastings.

Harold gathered his infantry on Senlac Hill. Attacking uphill with cavalry and archers (*below*), William won a spectacular victory. The age of the knight had arrived.

Ob-Ugrians
The feared 11th-century Ugrian horsemen (right) *came from the icy regions of northern Europe. They carried simple yet deadly bows and ring-pommel swords.*

BULL'S EYE. The Bayeux Tapestry (20 inches wide and 230 feet long) was embroidered in Normandy and records Duke William's seizure of the English throne (*above right*). The tapestry is responsible for the myth of Harold being killed by an arrow in the eye – in reality he was struck down by four Norman knights.

Huns (below center)
Tribes of Mongol Huns swept into Western Europe in the late 4th century A.D. *Brilliant horsemen, they settled in Hungary and even reached the gates of Rome.*

THE KNIGHT'S CODE

Charlemagne (*left*, A.D. 768-814), king of the Franks and the first Holy Roman Emperor, acquired an empire that stretched from Spain to Poland.

At the heart of his armies were rich and privileged knights. They developed a code of conduct toward each other that became known as "chivalry."

Avars
An Avar horseman of the 7th century A.D. *(left). The Avars, a nomadic Tatar people from central Asia, were part of the second wave of invaders from central Asia. They settled in the region north of the Black Sea.*

Arab cavalry
was mounted on small but fast ponies.

MARTEL'S METHOD

Using heavily-armored cavalrymen, Charles Martel halted the Muslim invasion of Europe at the Battle of Poitiers in A.D. 732.

He rewarded his knights with land to live on. This system – land in exchange for service – later developed into feudalism (page 28).

Anglo-Saxon infantry
(above) *defend bravely against a Norman cavalry charge.*

William the Conqueror (left) *was the son of a tanner's daughter. He died while he was duke of Normandy and king of England. He was one of Europe's most powerful rulers.*

THE AGE OF THE KNIGHT

Between about 900 and 1400 the mounted knight was the most valued European battle weapon. Knights were more than just warriors. They formed a privileged group at the top of society. The division of land was geared to the cost of putting an armored knight into the field and knightly behavior, known as *chivalry*, was held up as an example for everyone to follow.

Nevertheless, the importance of mounted knights in battle is easily exaggerated. They looked magnificent and could make devastating charges. But medieval warfare was primarily about capturing enemy castles, not cavalry attacks.

Commanders usually avoided battle if they could. Besides, in an extended fight a knight with his head inside a steel helmet often had no idea what was going on!

A SOLDIER OF FORTUNE

Until 1300, some lords paid for their knights' equipment, but as the cost of armor and a war horse rose, the practice stopped.

Soon being a knight cost an arm and a leg in more ways than one. The enormous expense of putting an armored, mounted warrior in the field restricted knighthood to all but the wealthiest families.

Knight in 1200

CASTLES COUNT!

Large-scale battles between mounted knights were rare and usually of little significance.

The capture of mighty Château-Gaillard from French King John (*above*) in 1204, for example, had more impact on the history of France than any cavalry conflict.

Château-Gaillard (above) *dominated the countryside for miles around.*

The Sword in the Stone
British director John Boorman used the name Excalibur – *Arthur's magical sword (right) – as the title of his remake of the legend (left).*

Arthur found the weapon sticking into a stone and returned it to the Lady of the Lake when he died.

THE LEGEND OF KING ARTHUR is a blend of ancient British and French myth, spiced with Christianity, and a dash of fact.

The real Arthur may have been a Romano-Briton who fought the Anglo-Saxon invaders in the 6th century A.D.

Arthur, the romantic hero of Camelot was created by the 12th-century monk Geoffrey of Monmouth.

Geoffrey set the tales in his own time, with his own religious message. This is why they feature knights in armor, Christian chivalry, and glamorous ladies in long pointed hats!

The Power of the Sword
The sword, ideal for stabbing and slashing, was the basic weapon of every knight.

Knight in 1500

CHAOS AT BOUVINES (*above*)
King John lost his French possessions with the fall of Château-Gaillard (page 14).

When he tried to get them back, he was heavily defeated in 1214 at Bouvines, Flanders (modern Belgium).

The battle was a rare example of a major conflict between mounted knights. After the first assault, the fight deteriorated into total chaos!

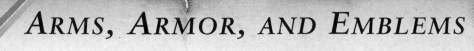

ARMS, ARMOR, AND EMBLEMS

A 14th-century knight carried a three-foot-long sword, a triangular shield, a lance, and a thin dagger. For hand-to-hand fighting the lance was replaced by an axe or spiked club, known as a mace. A well-directed axe could divide the skull of a giant war horse! Knights wore chain mail (page 17) and plate armor to protect against the cuts and blows of a sword or mace – but it didn't stop them from getting very badly bruised. They even protected their horses with mail, leather, plates, or quilts (*below*). When fighting on foot, knights often swapped their large iron helmets for those that did not cover their faces, so they could see what was going on. Wrapped up in all that metal, leather, and cloth, a knight grew too hot and thirsty to fight for long, especially in the summer!

1100

1225

1350

1450

1500

Heavy metal? It is complete fiction that knights had to be craned onto their horses! Full armor weighed no more than about 40 pounds and was actually quite flexible to walk around in.

The first iron plate armor was in use by the 13th century. The main pieces were breastplates and backplates, collars, and arm and leg guards. Extra plates fitted over the shoulders, elbows, and knees.

NICE HELMET!
Just as chain mail was replaced by plate armor, so helmet styles changed to provide better protection (and sometimes just to look good, *left*).

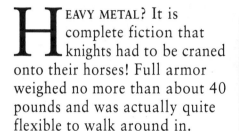

Dressing for Battle
A squire helps his master dress for battle (main picture). Each piece of plate armor had to be carefully buckled into place over the suit of chain mail, so dressing could take over an hour.

Chain mail was made of thousands of iron rings. These were linked together in a pattern a bit like knitting (left)! A knight wore a chain mail tunic, called a "hauberk" over padded undergarments. He also put on chain mail leggings, gauntlets, and a balaclava known as a "coif."

COAT OF ARMS

Coats of arms were originally loose coats worn over armor. As they came to carry a knight's emblem or "arms," the emblem itself became known as a "coat of arms." As the pictures on the *right* show (from top to bottom), when families intermarried they combined their coats of arms:

I A lord (*with the blue and yellow coat of arms*) has no son, but his daughter marries a lord with the red and white coat.
II The coats are combined (called *impaling*).
III When the lady's father dies, the coat of arms changes again.
IV When the lady's husband dies, the son has the coat of arms quartered, or divided into four.

HERALDRY

Heraldry is the system of coats of arms. It developed from the emblems that knights used to identify themselves in battle (*below*). It also helped a herald (who also designed the coat) to work out who had died in battle.

I

II

III

IV

Arms in a Tangle!
In time the number of heraldic designs grew so complex that a College of Arms was set up to decide who had which coat of arms.

17

SOLDIERS OF GOD

In the summer of 1095 Pope Urban II was at Clermont, in central France. There, before a huge crowd, he preached a momentous sermon. The Holy Places of the East, he declared, had fallen into the hands of the infidel. All who helped free them would be forgiven their sins!

Urban's sermon launched the First Crusade (*left*). A religious war was just what Europe's knights had been waiting for. Thousands made their way to the Holy Land. By 1100 the Turks had been defeated, Jerusalem recaptured, and four "crusader states" set up. Seven crusades followed. All were bloody, few were successful. By 1291 the great fortress of Acre, the last Christian stronghold in Syria, had been lost. Ultimately, the knights had failed their greatest challenge.

HOLY IN-SPEAR-ATION
In 1098, when Crusader fortunes were running low, a young man named Peter Bartholomew had a vision of the Holy Lance that had pierced Christ's side buried beneath a church in Antioch.

Digging began and, sure enough, an old spear (*left*) was uncovered. Inspired by the relic, the Crusaders went on to take Jerusalem.

Bloodbath!
The month-long siege of Jerusalem ended on July 15, 1099, when the holy city fell to the crusader knights in a slaughtering spree (right).

One report claimed that after the slaughter the knights rode through blood so deep that it covered their horses' knees.

THE KNIGHT OF ISLAM

The Muslim soldier and ruler Salah al-Din – Saladin (*left*) – recaptured Jerusalem in 1187. In stark contrast to Christian bloodthirstiness, he let the inhabitants depart in peace.

The Third Crusade, led by Richard the Lionheart, inflicted several defeats on Saladin, but failed to take back Jerusalem. Finally, the two great warriors signed a truce giving Christian pilgrims access to the Holy Sepulcher.

Under Siege (main picture)
The importance of a siege is shown by the price attackers were willing to pay – tens of thousands of Crusaders died taking the city of Acre.

Lionhearted Dick?
Richard I (above) is often portrayed as a Christian hero, but he happily butchered 2,700 prisoners after the fall of Acre in 1191.

KNIGHTS TEMPLAR

The Knights of the Holy Temple in Jerusalem were an order of professional crusaders (*above left*). Based in Cyprus, they fought in several crusades and became extremely prosperous. Philip IV of France disbanded the order in 1307 to get his hands on its wealth.

El CID. Rodrigo de Vivar, "El Cid" (meaning "the lord"), was the ultimate Spanish hero. He became a legend in his own lifetime (1043-1099) because he never lost a battle.

He also fought against both Christians and Muslims, so he was hardly an ideal Crusader. This was quietly forgotten in the film starring Charlton Heston (*left*).

THE MIGHT OF THE MONGOLS

European knights fought well on their own, or in small groups, but as part of an army their lack of discipline frequently made them liabilities. This was in sharp contrast to the disciplined Mongol cavalry of Genghis Khan and his successors – the greatest conquerors the world has ever known.

Apart from a siege train, a Mongol army consisted almost entirely of cavalry. The light cavalry were armed with bows and arrows and knives or swords, and wore only a helmet for protection. Like their European counterparts, the heavy cavalry wore armor and carried lances. The Mongol tactic was to bombard the enemy line with arrows, then charge with heavy cavalry when a weakness appeared.

KHAN THE CONQUEROR

Genghis Khan's father was the chief of a small Mongol tribe, but by 1206 Genghis was recognized as *khan* (leader) of all the Mongols and "the lord of all peoples dwelling in felt tents." He immediately reorganized his forces and set his goal – to conquer the world! China came first.

After taking vast areas of the north of the country, he swept west through Turkestan, Persia, northern India, and southern Russia.

MARE'S MILK
The soldiers of Genghis Khan were expected to live off the land. Most of the cavalry rode mares, so they could drink the mare's milk (*left*).

Saddle Shooters
Mongol light cavalry in action with their deadly bows and arrows (above). They sharpened their skills by hunting for food.

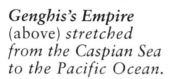

Genghis's Empire (above) *stretched from the Caspian Sea to the Pacific Ocean.*

THE DECIMAL DESTROYERS
The key to Mongol success was organization. Ten squads of ten men made a squadron of 100 men, and ten squadrons a regiment of 1,000 men. Ten battalions made up a *touman*. Signals passed between the men by means of shouts, flags, and flaming arrows.

No Mercy
The Mongol armies (above) *ruthlessly eliminated all opposition. They spread terror and destruction everywhere. If any resistance was encountered, they butchered the populations of entire cities.*

EAST VS WEST
The Mongol cavalry met the Christian knights at the battle of Liegnitz, Hungary in 1241.

The result was a resounding victory for the invading Mongols.

WINTER WAR
Batu, a grandson of Genghis, directed the Mongol invasion of Europe of 1237-1240. It began with a brilliant winter invasion of Russia, the only time in history that Russia has been successfully attacked at the harshest time of year.

Using the frozen rivers as highways, 150,000 Mongols swept over the Volga and captured Moscow (*right*). Kiev fell two years later.

SAMURAI WARRIORS

The samurai were the knights of Japan. They emerged as mounted peacekeepers in the 9th century, fighting with swords and bows and arrows. Like European knights, they were bound by a code of honor, known as *bushido*.

By the 12th century, two samurai families, the Taira and the Minamoto, were among the most powerful in Japan. In 1185, Minamoto Yoritomo set up his own government in the emperor's name. When he was appointed *shogun* (commander-in-chief) in 1192, he sent out samurai warriors to govern the provinces.

For 650 years after Yoritomo's death, the Samurai dominated many aspects of Japan's social, artistic, economic, and religious life. Even when feudal Japan collapsed, *bushido* remained a powerful moral code.

Samurai Armor
The samurai did not wear plate armor until the arrival of firearms in the 16th century.

Before that, they wore highly decorated, flexible armor made of leather, mail, and metal scales (below).

Toyotomi Hideyoshi (1539-1598, above), the first person to unify all of Japan, began his career as a foot soldier.

THE WARRIOR'S WAY
"The Way of the Warrior" or *bushido*, was similar to chivalry. Both began as warrior codes, praising loyalty and bravery, even to death.

As chivalry drew from Christianity, so *bushido* drew from Confucianism. When not fighting, the samurai *shih* (gentleman) was expected to be courteous, artistic, and noble.

KNOWN BY YOUR **POEM.** The samurai equivalent of heraldry was *sashimono*. Each warrior was identified by the small flag that was attached to his back (*right*). On one side of the flag he sometimes wrote a poem. One tribe shared the same poem. Only when they were all gathered together could it be read,

Colors smell sweetly, but they will fade.
Nothing in the world lasts forever...

Sashimono
Three examples of the personal flags worn by samurai (below).

SLAVES TO THE SAMURAI

In medieval Japan, women were even less well regarded than in medieval Europe. They were expected to be totally subservient to their husbands, dying for them if necessary. They were often forced into arranged marriages to increase the power of their families.

Kabuki *plays often retold tales of heroic samurai (below). Like Shakespearean theater, all women's roles were played by men or boys.*

A Female Warrior (main picture) *Tomoe Gozen, the heroic wife of Minamoto Yoshinaka, is one of the few samurai women whose reputation as a fighter matched that of her husband.*

FOOT SOLDIERS FIGHT BACK

It is autumn, 1415. Henry V and his army of 6,000 are desperate. Sick, tired, and soaked by torrential rain, they struggle to reach Calais. But there is no escape. On October 19, they find a French army of some 40,000 men blocking their path home.

The French arrange their forces in a narrow field surrounded by woods. It seems only a matter of time before their huge army of knights crushes the English into the mud.

But the mud is Henry's ally. The French chivalry struggle to mount an effective charge. First, their own foot soldiers get in the way. Then the horses start sliding all over the place. Finally, like a gigantic swarm of bees, a rain of deadly arrows starts to fall among them.

Three hours later, 5,000 Frenchmen lie dead on the Agincourt field.

A PRICKLY OPPONENT
Since the time of the Macedonian shock infantry (*top*) the pike had been the foot soldier's best defense against cavalry.

The pike was a very long pole with a metal spike on the end. When held together in large numbers they resembled a huge hedgehog (*below*).

A halberd (see main picture) had a shorter handle than the pike, with an axe blade on one side and a hook or spike on the other.

Sitting Duck (main picture)
His horse wounded by an arrow, a French knight comes crashing to the ground. Unless he moves quickly, the English infantry will capture him and cut his throat.

SLAUGHTER AT AGINCOURT
Some 1,500 French knights, the finest of the country's chivalry, were among the dead – Henry V lost perhaps only 100 men. So even before gunpowder had made its mark, the age of the knight was drawing to a close.

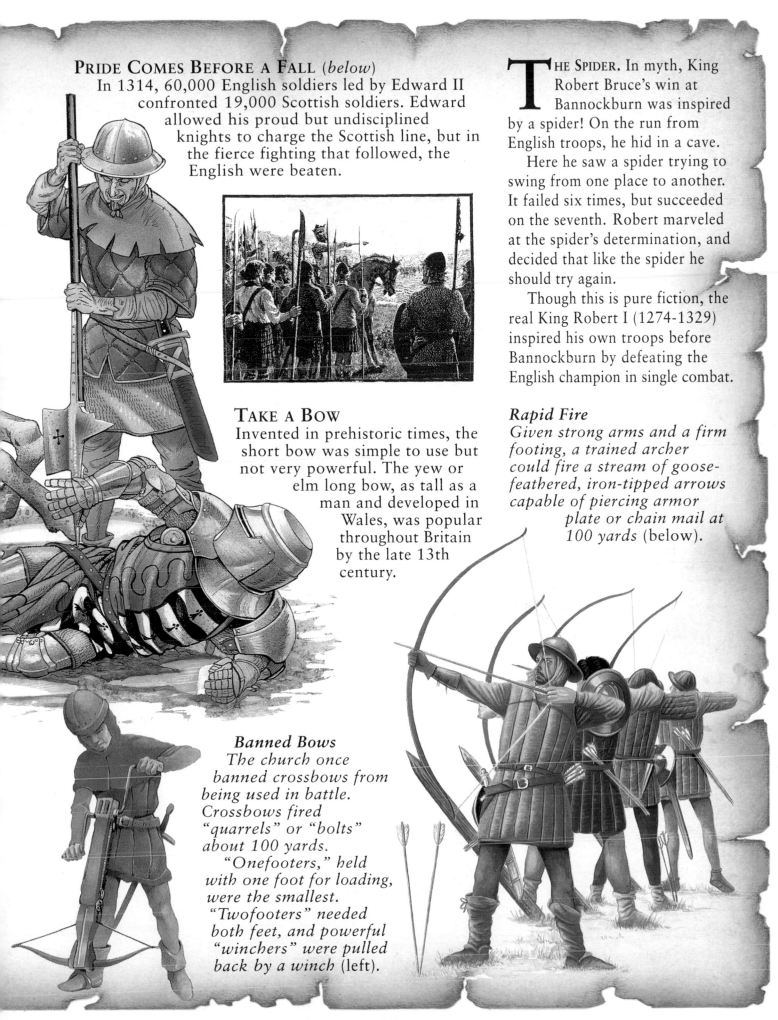

PRIDE COMES BEFORE A FALL (*below*)

In 1314, 60,000 English soldiers led by Edward II confronted 19,000 Scottish soldiers. Edward allowed his proud but undisciplined knights to charge the Scottish line, but in the fierce fighting that followed, the English were beaten.

TAKE A BOW

Invented in prehistoric times, the short bow was simple to use but not very powerful. The yew or elm long bow, as tall as a man and developed in Wales, was popular throughout Britain by the late 13th century.

Banned Bows

The church once banned crossbows from being used in battle. Crossbows fired "quarrels" or "bolts" about 100 yards.

"Onefooters," held with one foot for loading, were the smallest. "Twofooters" needed both feet, and powerful "winchers" were pulled back by a winch (left).

THE SPIDER. In myth, King Robert Bruce's win at Bannockburn was inspired by a spider! On the run from English troops, he hid in a cave.

Here he saw a spider trying to swing from one place to another. It failed six times, but succeeded on the seventh. Robert marveled at the spider's determination, and decided that like the spider he should try again.

Though this is pure fiction, the real King Robert I (1274-1329) inspired his own troops before Bannockburn by defeating the English champion in single combat.

Rapid Fire

Given strong arms and a firm footing, a trained archer could fire a stream of goose-feathered, iron-tipped arrows capable of piercing armor plate or chain mail at 100 yards (below).

CHIVALRY

The word "knight" comes from the Old English word *Cniht*, meaning a servant. The French equivalent is *chevalier*, from which we get the knightly code of behavior known as "chivalry."

Chivalry, originally a pact among privileged soldiers, developed from the time of Charlemagne. It reached its height in the 14th and 15th centuries, when there were many "orders" of chivalry, such as the Templars and the Knights of St. John.

Chivalry required knights to be brave, honorable, loyal, and generous. It also owed much to Christianity and medieval "romances." These were tales of knights' pure devotion to the damsels they loved. The romantic ideal helped raise the status of women and change the barbarous image of knights.

GIRDING THE SWORD

A young man went through an elaborate ritual to become a knight. Today we think of the monarch tapping a knight on the head and shoulders, but during the Middle Ages the heart of the ceremony was the moment when he fastened (girded) his sword (*below*).

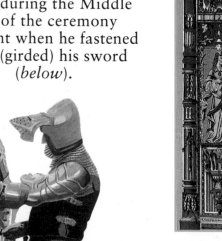

GEORGIUS

GEORGE AND THE DRAGON. St. George was an early Christian martyr. By the Middle Ages, he had become a hero of chivalry, famous for rescuing a fair maiden from a fiery dragon (*above*).

In 1348, Edward III made St. George patron saint of his new Order of the Garter, the highest order of English chivalry. St. George has been England's national saint ever since.

Courtly Love
The aristocratic ideal of courtly love beheld the lover knight as humble, true, and utterly devoted to a haughty and chaste lady (below).

WINNING HIS SPURS

Before their crushing defeat at Crécy (1346), the French knights arrogantly regarded the English foot soldiers as inferior.

Ironically, Edward III's son the Black Prince won his spurs (*right*) – a symbol of knighthood – for his performance in the battle as a foot soldier.

GAWAIN AND THE GREEN KNIGHT. This fine medieval poem tells how Sir Gawain beheads a gigantic green knight, who then picks up his head and rides off. Within a year Sir Gawain has to receive a similar blow himself.

When he resists temptation and offers his head to the Green Knight's axe, he is saved for remaining true to the code of chivalry (*right*).

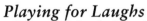

The Ultimate Quest
The Holy Grail was the cup Jesus drank from at the Last Supper. It was then used to catch his blood as it dropped from the cross.

By medieval times there were numerous legends, some using pre-Christian stories, of knights looking for this Holy Grail. The Grail has been featured in many stories, and even the film Indiana Jones and the Last Crusade.

Playing for Laughs
The world of chivalry is so remote from our own that it is easy to poke fun at it. One of the first to do so was Mark Twain, in A Connecticut Yankee in King Arthur's Court.

More recently, the comedy films Monty Python and the Holy Grail *(above) and* Jabberwocky *(right) have laughed at myths of King Arthur and tales of knights, dragons, and damsels in distress.*

FEUDALISM

No one sat down and worked out a "feudal system." It developed as a way of life, an agreement between lord and master. Essentially, the lord gave land and protection in return for service and loyalty.

The king owned all the land. He gave it out in "fiefs" to his barons. In return for this land, protection, and various other privileges, such as the right to run law courts and raise taxes, the baron swore allegiance to the king.

The barons also undertook to provide a number of "knight services" or "castle guards" when required. They exchanged land and protection for service with knights. And so the "feudal pyramid" grew, increasing the number of serfs at the bottom.

CHAUCER'S TALES. Geoffrey Chaucer's Canterbury Tales (begun in about 1387 and finished in 1400) tells how pilgrims traveling from London to the shrine of St. Thomas Becket in Canterbury told each other stories to pass the time.

The chief pilgrim, who told his tale first, was a "very perfect, gentle" knight (*left*), who "loved chivalry, truth and honor, freedom, and courtesy."

GOING DOWN

Never perfect, the feudal system soon grew corrupt. Money replaced service because paid soldiers fought better than the "feudal levy." Given that they were sometimes trampled to death by their own knights, it is no wonder that serfs often refused to fight.

Chess – with its kings, queens, bishops, knights, and castles – is like a game about the feudal system (right)*! Brought to Spain by the Muslim invaders, by* A.D. *1000 it had spread through Europe. (An 11th century piece is* left).

Someone To Watch Over You
The feudal system is reflected in this medieval illustration – peasants labor in the fields under the protection (and watchful eye) of the lord in his castle.

MEN FOR MONEY
According to feudalism, soldiers fought out of duty to their lord. In time, lords found they got better soldiers if they took money ("scutage") instead of military service. They used the cash to hire mercenaries – professional soldiers – to do the fighting.

The Great Charter
In the document known as Magna Carta (1215) King John confirmed the privileges of the knightly class. Later, the privileges were applied to all (below).

A TRAIL OF BROKEN PROMISES
One of the few powerful medieval women was the Empress Matilda. She was the only surviving child of English King Henry I, who got all his barons to promise to accept Matilda as his heir. But when Henry died in 1135, many barons broke their word (so much for their chivalry!) because they refused to be ruled by a woman.

Stephen of Blois saw a chance to seize the throne. A civil war followed and was so cruel that, according to one source, "God and his angels slept."

Medieval men believed women were inferior. They saw marriages as business deals and women's main job as producing children. Many couples were married at fourteen.

KNIGHTS AND CASTLES

The castle had many purposes. It was a home for the lord, his family, and servants; it was a symbol of his power, dominating all other buildings in the area apart from the church; it was a store for weapons and food; and it was a refuge in times of danger.

In medieval times land was wealth. A castle defended that wealth and so was as important to a king or baron as his knights. The first castles consisted of a keep on a large mound (the motte) surrounded by a walled lower area (the bailey). The walls were wood or stone. From the 1270s onward, all-stone castles such as Harlech in Wales (*main picture*) were built with rings of walls and towers. Before gunpowder, a well-built castle like this could take weeks to subdue.

CASTLES OF DELIGHT

Castles in Japan were built differently from those in Europe. The samurai did not produce the West's advanced siege weapons and techniques, and they were more concerned with individual prowess in the battlefield than with the static slog of siege warfare.

As a result, samurai castles, like samurai armor, were works of art. Placed on hilltops and decorated with sweeping roofs and elegant windows, they were a joy to behold (*below*) as well as useful refuges in times of war.

Guard the Door! During the 13th century it became common to combine gatehouse (a castle's weakest point) and keep in one massive fortification.

Preparing for a Long Siege Women and servants are led while the castle stocks up on food, drink, medical suppli and ammunition.

Duffus Castle in Scotland (above) *is an example of a Norman motte and bailey castle.*

Pure Disney – *the castle at Disneyland, Paris wouldn't last long in a siege (below)!*

Hoarding
In preparation for a siege, an overhanging wooden hoarding, covered in damp hide for protection against fire, was attached along the tops of the walls and on turrets (top).

This sheltered the defending soldiers. It also allowed them to drop rocks and boiling oil on the attackers below (right).

To Take A Castle:
1. Simply surround it and force the garrison to surrender through starvation.
2. Set it alight with fire arrows. Or fling burning rags over the walls.
3. Dig a mine beneath the walls. Support the roof with wooden props. Set fire to them, to bring down the tunnel and the walls.
4. Knock holes in the defenses with battering rams or siege engines.
5. Storm the walls with ladders and towers.
6. Treachery!

Attacking Strategy
Attackers tried to drain the moat and fill it with dirt to allow their siege engines to get right up to the walls.

FISHY BUSINESS
Heddingham Castle's (*right*) system of secret passages beyond the walls enabled the besieged garrison to be supplied with food. Once, when fresh fish was thrown at attackers, they realized the castle would be starved into submission.

IN THE LISTS

In 1292, Edward I of England (*left*) drew up a statute which he hoped would stop unnecessary injury during tournaments. But 300 years later, jousting was still a dangerous game!

Astrologers had long predicted that King Henry II of France would meet an untimely end. The warnings worried the court and the queen, but the hearty 40-year-old king was not alarmed.

In the summer of 1559, Henry was in a festive mood. Calais had just been returned to France after 211 years in English hands. To celebrate, he organized a jousting tournament at Tournelles. Being fit and athletic, Henry joined in. It was not a sensible move. His opponent's lance broke, a large splinter drove into his head above the right eye, and within a few days he was dead.

Today's Jouster (above) *practicing in the traditional way, with a target attached to a swiveling pole.*

FREE-FOR-ALL

The first tournaments were fought by two teams of 40-50 knights. These fights were much like real battles, and could last all day!

In 1130, Pope Innocent II banned tournaments as a danger to life and limb, and even refused Christian burial to anyone who died in a tournament.

But no one took the ban seriously. In fact, Richard the Lionheart encouraged tournaments, because he thought his knights needed the practice!

Lances could be very dangerous if they split or hit a rival in the throat.

War Horse
A knight's horse was by far his most important piece of equipment (above). It was also the most expensive. A fine war horse cost more than many people earned in a lifetime.

THE TOURNAMENT

By the 1200s the bloody and wasteful clashes between many knights were replaced by jousting. This was governed by much stricter rules (*above*).

For a mounted challenge the field (the "lists") was divided by a low fence, or "tilt." Announced by heralds, two knights charged each other with blunted lances (*main picture*). The winner won by knocking his opponent out of his saddle.

Do Me a Favor!
The joust became a social gathering attended by ladies and a large crowd of common people.

Before the joust, knights would sometimes receive a ribbon or scarf (above) *known as a favor* from one of the watching ladies.

They were now the lady's champion and fought the joust with the scarf tied to their arm, a symbol of their devotion to the lady.

Armor was heavy, highly decorated, and topped with a helmet with very restricted vision.

THE THUNDER OF GUNS

When guns were first introduced in the early 14th century, they had more influence on siege warfare than battle tactics. By 1425, there was not a castle that could not be battered into swift submission by cannon fire.

Armored knights hung on longer. The final proof that they were no longer needed came at the Battle of Ravenna (1512), when French cannons destroyed a large Spanish army. By the 17th century, the wide use of handguns meant that armor was all but stripped away (*left*).

Chivalric ideals survived, however. Knightly honors were given for feats of bravery and other services, and chivalric orders, such as the Burgundian Order of the Golden Fleece, were still admired.

HAIL THE MIGHTY CANNON

The first cannons were cast from bronze, brass, or iron bars. Gunpowder, a mixture of charcoal, potassium nitrate, and sulfur was made on the spot because of the danger of transporting it.

The gun was loaded by pouring powder down the barrel and holding it in place with wadding. A cannon ball was then rolled down the barrel and secured with more wadding.

To fire the gun (above) *the gunpowder was lit through a small hole in the rear. The explosion blasted the ball out of the barrel toward its target. Gunners were protected from arrows by a wooden screen.*

Watch Out for the Big Bang!
Gunners cover their ears from the blast (above). In the early days, cannons frequently exploded upon firing. Also, the ignition of the slow-burning powder was so random that accuracy was almost impossible.

A TUDOR SUMMIT

Though knights were no longer a powerful force on the battlefield, many of the traditions and customs survived.

In 1520, King Henry VIII led the elite of English chivalry to meet the elite of Francis I's French knights on the Field of the Cloth of Gold *(left)*.

By now the jousting and feasting were supposed to demonstrate Anglo-French friendship, rather than a show of military force.

Fantasy Land
Scholars believe the original Camelot was in the English counties of Cornwall, Hampshire, or Somerset.

None of this is relevant to the musical Camelot, *which places the court of King Arthur in a singing and dancing medieval fantasy land* (right)*!*

DON QUIXOTE. Miguel de Cervantes Saavedra mirrored the decline of Spanish chivalry in his two-part novel *Don Quixote de la Mancha* (1605-1615). It is a story about a Spanish landowner who adores tales of the knights of old. Wishing to live like the knights, he takes the name Don Quixote and sets out to perform great deeds of chivalry, accompanied by his loyal friend Sancho Panza *(left)*.

Don Quixote attacks windmills he thinks are giants and flocks of sheep he mistakes for armies! When all his adventures prove romantic follies, he returns home to die.

Arise, Sir Francis!
No longer was the honor of knight reserved for mounted warriors. When Francis Drake returned from sailing around the world, on April 4, 1581 *Queen Elizabeth knighted him on board his ship* (right)*. He hadn't been near a horse for almost three years!*

THE CAVALRY

The arrival of firearms destroyed the effectiveness of the mounted knight in open battle. Gone were the days of the galloping charge into terrified infantry – a man on a horse was a huge and vulnerable target for both cannon and musket fire.

Nevertheless, a horse was still the fastest means of travel. All armies needed mobile forces for scouting, outflanking, pursuit, and covering withdrawal. This led to the replacement of the small elite force of knights with the massed ranks of the cavalry.

Because horses were expensive, only the rich could afford to join the cavalry, but they now had to train and submit to orders along with the other men. Cavalry was divided into light and heavy, with dragoons (*above*) making up a third force.

Austrian Dragoons (right) *get into position during the Seven Years' War (1756-1763). A musket could only be reloaded once the user had dismounted* (left).

FLAMING DRAGONS

Dragoons were originally mounted infantry armed with a short French musket, known as a dragon, which they usually dismounted to fire. Dragoons kept their name after the dragon had gone out of service.

A Brutal Chopper

The main cavalry weapon was the saber. This was a curved sword with a single cutting edge, ideal for slashing from horseback (left). *The straighter saber used by heavy cavalry was not built for the clever swordplay often seen in the movies: troopers were simply taught to aim for the opponent's left ear.*

Dragoon Musket

DOYLE'S HUSSAR
Sir Arthur Conan Doyle, creator of the famous detective Sherlock Holmes, also wrote *The Exploits of Brigadier Gerard,* about a heroic French hussar officer fighting in Napoléon's army.

Hussars were light cavalry in colorful uniforms (page 42), originally from Hungary.

THE GREAT SWEDE
Gustavus Adolphus (1595-1630, *left*) was the first commander to fully integrate cavalry into his army. They were treated as an arm of his forces, not as a privileged or special unit, and operated closely with the infantry and artillery.

NOT SO DARING! Some pictures of 16th century cavalry show them charging at their opponents with reckless abandon. In reality the standard tactic was a *caracole* – riding up to the enemy, firing a single shot, then retreating. Hardly the stuff of heroes!

FORM SQUARES!
In Napoleonic times the standard infantry defense against cavalry was to form a square (*above*). To increase firepower, soldiers in the front rank, on the outside of the square, knelt and those behind them stood. Men retreated inward to reload. A square's main weakness was its vulnerability to cannon fire.

Cavalry Sword

Napoleonic cavalry (right) *is usually depicted in smart, orderly uniforms, but in reality most troopers paid little attention to dress rules and were often covered in mud. The Duke of Wellington once banned his cavalry from carrying umbrellas in battle!*

*Aztec
Knights*
Although without horses, the Aztecs had their knights – the Jaguar and Eagle warriors (top). *They wore thick armor of quilted cotton and fought with clublike swords edged with a hard volcanic glass.*

A SPANISH SUN GOD

Hernán Cortéz (*above*) led an army of 600 Spaniards into Aztec lands in 1519.

Not having seen white men, guns, or horses before, at first the Aztecs thought Cortéz was a sun god. By 1521 he had seized their empire and destroyed their capital city.

THE CONQUISTADORS

In 1530, Spaniards exploring the region of modern Peru came across the Inca Empire. Immensely rich, but without wheels or writing, this highly organized state had existed for 1,000 years. Conquistador (conqueror) Francisco Pizarro determined to make this empire his own.

He set out in 1531 with 63 horsemen and 200 foot soldiers. The Incas had not seen firearms or horses before. With an incredible display of bravery and bloodthirsty cunning, Pizarro's ruthless band of "knights of the New World" (*below*) made themselves masters of 10 million Incas within a year.

CHRISTIAN SOLDIERS?

The Spaniards were shocked when they found that captives of the Aztecs were sacrificed to their gods (*left*), but the conquistadors hardly behaved like chivalrous knights either.

Once in power, Spanish rule was marked by acts of savage butchery. One local king was dragged behind a horse then burned alive, and thousands of American Indians were rounded up then worked to death in the mines.

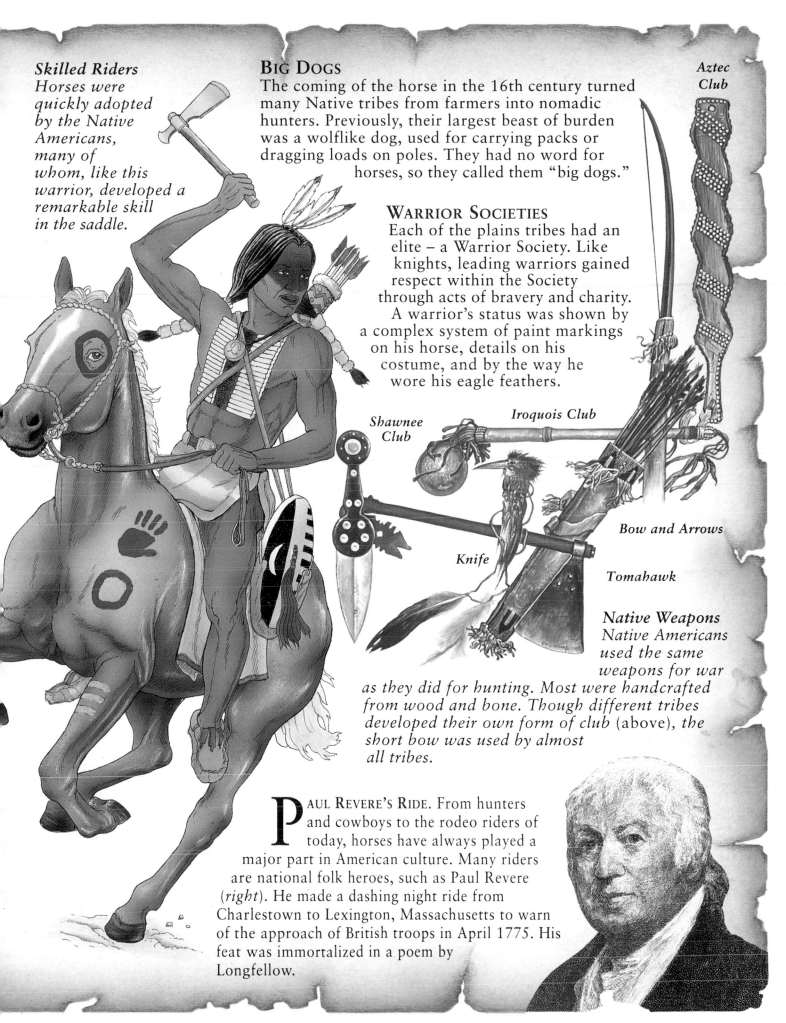

Skilled Riders
Horses were quickly adopted by the Native Americans, many of whom, like this warrior, developed a remarkable skill in the saddle.

BIG DOGS

The coming of the horse in the 16th century turned many Native tribes from farmers into nomadic hunters. Previously, their largest beast of burden was a wolflike dog, used for carrying packs or dragging loads on poles. They had no word for horses, so they called them "big dogs."

WARRIOR SOCIETIES

Each of the plains tribes had an elite – a Warrior Society. Like knights, leading warriors gained respect within the Society through acts of bravery and charity. A warrior's status was shown by a complex system of paint markings on his horse, details on his costume, and by the way he wore his eagle feathers.

Aztec Club

Shawnee Club

Iroquois Club

Bow and Arrows

Knife

Tomahawk

Native Weapons
Native Americans used the same weapons for war as they did for hunting. Most were handcrafted from wood and bone. Though different tribes developed their own form of club (above), the short bow was used by almost all tribes.

PAUL REVERE'S RIDE. From hunters and cowboys to the rodeo riders of today, horses have always played a major part in American culture. Many riders are national folk heroes, such as Paul Revere (*right*). He made a dashing night ride from Charlestown to Lexington, Massachusetts to warn of the approach of British troops in April 1775. His feat was immortalized in a poem by Longfellow.

COSSACKS AND LANCERS

The Cossacks (*left*) were descendants of the Asian invaders that had moved westward in the Middle Ages. Like their ancestors, they were brilliant horsemen and their regiments were the most feared in the Russian Army. They were also a fiercely independent people and many left the USSR after fighting the Communists in the Civil War of 1917-1922.

By this time the importance of cavalry was declining sharply. But not until after World War II were mounted troops reserved just for ceremonial occasions.

During World War I both sides kept large cavalry forces behind the front lines, waiting for a breakthrough. As late as 1939 most armies, particularly the British Indian Army, still had active cavalry.

THE REBEL PUGACHEV
The war veteran Yemelyan Pugachev who pretended to be the assassinated husband of Tsarina Catherine stirred up a massive Cossack rebellion in 1773-1775. He was eventually captured, taken to Moscow in an iron cage, (*left*) and executed.

A COSSACK DANCE
In recent times the Cossack traditions of athletic horsemanship and dance have been exported around the world as entertainment. The men *below* are performing an exhausting traditional dance!

PUKKA SAHIBS

The Victorians were very proud of their Indian Army. Growing from the forces of the East India Company, it swelled into a huge army with a spectacular cavalry.

From Britain, thousands of miles away, the parades and brilliant uniforms appeared wonderful. But the army was not allowed to use artillery, in case of mutiny.

A Bengal Lancer (main picture)
The Bengal Lancers were recruited to police India's lawless northwest frontier.

Polo Mallet and Ball

JOLLY GOOD CHAPS!

The chivalric traditions of the aristocracy survive in the sport of polo.

Played only by men, it began in Iran and spread to India. Here it was taken up by young cavalry officers, who introduced it to England in 1869. Like hockey on horseback, the game tests a rider's skill to the limit.

An even more dangerous version is played in Mongolia, using an animal carcass as the "ball!"

Polo (left) remains a game for the rich!

BULLFIGHTING

Horsemen are crucial to the brutal Spanish sport of bullfighting. Riding horses that are protected from the bull's horns by leather armor, the *picadores* weaken the bull by piercing it with lances. Mounted *banderilleros* enrage the creature still further with darts, before the matador kills it with his sword (*right*).

Horse Gymnastics
The horse used in gymnastics today was originally designed so that cavalrymen could practice mounting their horse quickly!

"INTO THE VALLEY OF DEATH..."

In October 1854, during the Crimean War, the Russians began to advance on the British base at Balaclava. During the battle that followed, Lord Cardigan's Light Brigade received a mistaken instruction to capture some cannons at the end of a valley surrounded by enemy guns.

Trained to obey orders, however stupid, the 673 men of the Light Brigade set off. Ten minutes later, less than 200 returned.

When he read what had happened, the poet Tennyson wrote *The Charge of the Light Brigade*, making the incident sound almost glorious.

In fact, it was a scandalous example of how useless cavalry had become in attack. "Magnificent," noted a French observer, "but not war!"

The Dashing Hussar
Cavalry regiments have always regarded themselves as something special, as the splendid uniform of this British hussar (above) suggests. Even today, officers from British cavalry (tank) units are often from wealthy families.

THE BOYS IN BLUE. Few of history's mounted forces have been the subject of so much fiction as the United States cavalry. In countless movies the "boys in blue" are shown as brave, rugged, and independent, with the ability to appear over the brow of the hill to rescue innocent victims from Indian war parties, just when all seemed hopeless.

THE MYTH OF THE CAVALRY
In reality, the role of the U.S. cavalry in the 943 battles of Indian Wars of 1865-1898 was rarely glorious. The Sioux ambush of General Custer's 7th Cavalry at Little Big Horn (1876) was an example of incompetence that matched the British charge at Balaclava.

The Sand Creek massacre of 1864 showed another side of the cavalry, when a large force in Colorado attacked a village of peaceful Arapaho and Cheyenne and killed innocent men, women, and children alike (*left*).

The Charge of the Light Brigade
Charging the Russian cannons on a misunderstood order, the Light Brigade was shot at from three sides as they thundered to the end of the valley.

When the survivors finally reached the other end, they had no means of disabling the guns they had captured. To make matters worse, they then ran straight into the Russian cavalry (main picture)!

THE ARRIVAL OF THE IRON HORSE

Breech-loading rifles, cannons, and machine guns made the cavalry (*above*) far too vulnerable to play a major role in the set-piece battles of the Civil War (1861-1865). Horsemen were held back for guarding or pursuing.

In June 1863 J.E.B. Stuarts's Confederate 10,000 cavalry met 12,000 mounted Union troops. Yet even this titanic clash had little effect – two weeks later it was the infantry at Gettysburg that effectively settled the course of the war. Furthermore, the horse had a new rival. From now on, troops could be sped to the battlefield by the "iron horse" – the railway.

Polish Lancers, for all their bravery, had no chance against the guns and armor of German tanks (right).

The New Cavalry!
A World War I tank.

LANCERS VS PANZERS

The 20th-century equivalent of the knight in armor is the tank, and some regiments kept the name "cavalry" after they had converted to tanks. The German and Polish armies still had mounted cavalry when they met in 1939. The German generals immediately realized the pointlessness of a cavalry charge in modern warfare. The Poles did not, and their 11 cavalry brigades were slaughtered.

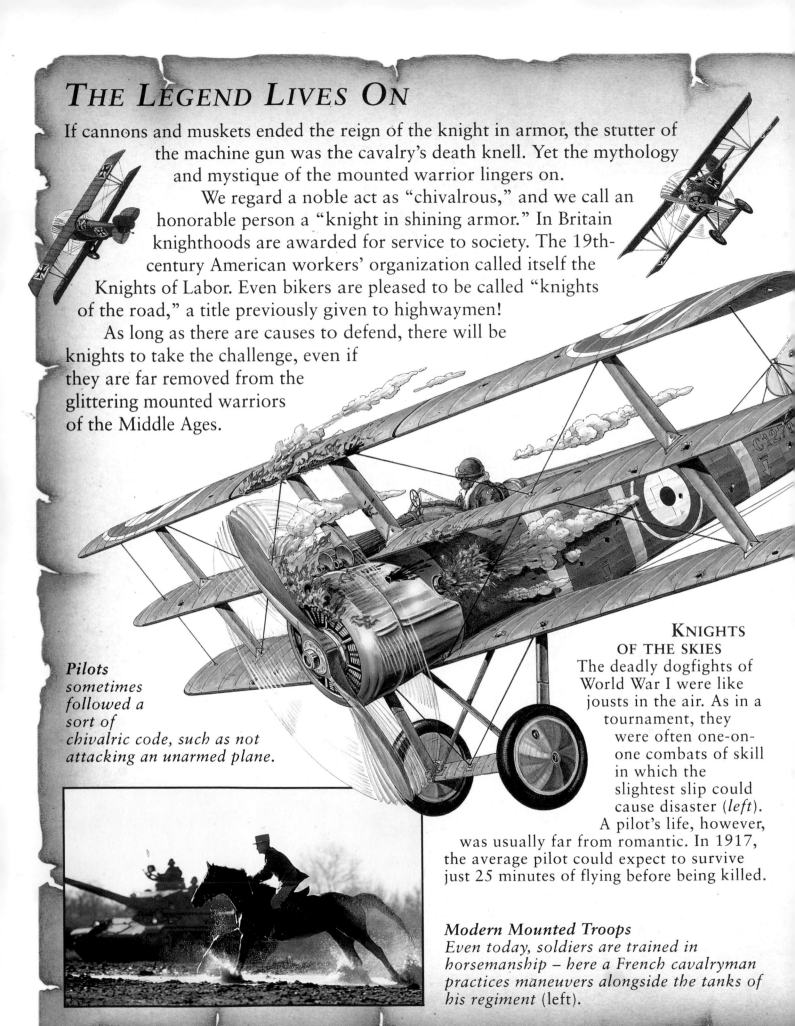

THE LEGEND LIVES ON

If cannons and muskets ended the reign of the knight in armor, the stutter of the machine gun was the cavalry's death knell. Yet the mythology and mystique of the mounted warrior lingers on.

We regard a noble act as "chivalrous," and we call an honorable person a "knight in shining armor." In Britain knighthoods are awarded for service to society. The 19th-century American workers' organization called itself the Knights of Labor. Even bikers are pleased to be called "knights of the road," a title previously given to highwaymen!

As long as there are causes to defend, there will be knights to take the challenge, even if they are far removed from the glittering mounted warriors of the Middle Ages.

Pilots sometimes followed a sort of chivalric code, such as not attacking an unarmed plane.

KNIGHTS OF THE SKIES

The deadly dogfights of World War I were like jousts in the air. As in a tournament, they were often one-on-one combats of skill in which the slightest slip could cause disaster (*left*). A pilot's life, however, was usually far from romantic. In 1917, the average pilot could expect to survive just 25 minutes of flying before being killed.

Modern Mounted Troops
Even today, soldiers are trained in horsemanship – here a French cavalryman practices maneuvers alongside the tanks of his regiment (left).

QUAINT HONORS

Twice a year the British Queen draws up a list of citizens to receive "honors." A handful join the Order of the Garter, an order of chivalry set up over 600 years ago for skill in jousting! Others become members of groups such as the Order of the Bath. Many more are made knights, though they have never held a sword or ridden a horse in their life!

Easy Riders
Independent-minded motorcyclists who travel the highways of the U.S. are known as "Knights of the Road." Their bikes (left) replace the horses of old.

Lords of the Manor
Some Scottish lairds still occupy the land and castles their family have owned since the Middle Ages (right).

S TAR WARS. When George Lucas's *Star Wars* hit the world's movie screens in 1977, it became the most successful film of all time. It also demonstrated the enduring strength of the knightly myth.

Although set in the future, the *Star Wars* trilogy has many of the features of the old Arthurian legends, including loyal and false knights, all-powerful swords (*left*), and hidden powers of good and bad magic.

POLICE KNIGHTS

Mounted police officers are used in many modern cities as they are ideally suited to dealing with large crowds. Perhaps the most famous are the red-jacketed Canadian Mounted Police, or "Mounties" (*right*). More than just law enforcement officers, they are living examples of the age-old fascination with warriors on horseback.

The Mounties – reputed always to "get their man" – are the subject of numerous legends.

THE LANGUAGE OF THE KNIGHT

Baggage train An army's baggage and supplies.

Bailey The lower walled enclosure of an early, Norman castle.

Baron A Feudal lord.

Breastplate The piece of armor covering the chest.

Bushido The code of honor of the Japanese Samurai.

Chain mail Armor made up of hundreds of interlinked loops of metal.

Chivalry The knight's code of conduct and honor.

Coat of arms A knight's personal emblem, originally worn on a vest over his armor.

Coif A helmet of chain mail.

Conquistador A Spanish explorer/conqueror of the New World (American continents).

Cossack Mounted warrior of south Russia.

Crusade Campaign by medieval Christians from Western Europe to recapture the Holy Land from the Muslim Turks.

Dragoon A mounted soldier equipped with firearms and sword, named after a short musket called the dragon (*above*).

Feudal system A system of sharing out land in return for service, usually military service.

Fodder Animal food.

Forage To look for food and fodder.

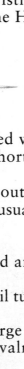

Hauberk Chain mail tunic.

Heavy cavalry Regiments with large horses used for cavalry charges.

Heraldry The system of designs and emblems by which armored knights were recognized (*left*).

Hilt Handle of a sword.

Holy Grail The cup in which Christ's blood was supposed to have been collected as it dripped from his crucified body.

Hussar Light cavalry, originally from Hungary.

Infantry Foot soldiers.

Infidel Unbeliever, a term used by Christian knights to describe their Muslim enemies.

Jousting Fighting with lances in a tournament.

Lance A long spear carried by cavalry.

Light cavalry Regiments with smaller, faster horses used for scouting and pursuing duties.

Lists The field where jousting was held.

Mercenary A soldier who fights for pay.

Motte The walled mound in a Norman castle.

Mountie A Royal Canadian Mounted Policeman.

Pilgrim One who travels to visit a holy shrine.

Pommel The knob on a saddle or on the hilt of a sword.

Reconnaissance A search of an area to see what's going on (i.e. to watch your enemies!).

Sally port A secret door/passage for getting out of a besieged castle.

Samurai The Japanese knightly class (*above*).

Scutage Payment in place of feudal service.

Shrine A place where holy relics (remains) are kept.

Siege train An army's siege weapons.

Spur Spikes worn on a rider's heel to control a horse (*above*).

Squire A knight's young assistant.

Tilt The fence between two jousting knights.

Tournament Organized fight before a crowd.

KNIGHTS TIMELINE

12,000 BC Humans first learn to train horses to work for them.

3000 BC Invention of the chariot (*left*) in the Middle East.

1479 BC Chariots take part in Meggido, world's first recorded battle .

776 BC Horse races mentioned in first Olympic Games.

c. 550 BC Persian king Cyrus the Great uses camels to defeat the Lydian king Croesus.

1st century AD Invention of the saddle.

218 AD Hannibal takes his elephants across the Alps.

378 AD Barbarian horsemen defeat the Romans at Adrianople.

4th century AD The stirrup is invented in China.

5th to 11th centuries Three separate waves of nomadic tribes (such as the Huns, *top right*) invade Europe from central Asia.

6th century Possible time of the real King Arthur, a Romano-British king.

7th to 10th centuries The Arabs build a Muslim empire from Spain to Persia.

8th–9th centuries Frankish kings Charles Martel and Charlemagne develop the early feudal system.

900 to 1400 Domination of the European battlefield by the knight and the rise of heraldry (*left*).

1040–1099 "El Cid" becomes a legend in his own lifetime.

1066 Anglo-Saxon foot soldiers are beaten by Norman knights at the Battle of Hastings.

1095 Pope Urban launches the First Crusade with his sermon at Clermont, France.

12th century Geoffrey of Monmouth creates the legend of King Arthur.

1185 Minamoto Yoritomo becomes shogun and begins 700 years of Samurai domination in Japan.

13th century Genghis Khan's mongols ride into Europe conquering all before them.

Mid-13th century Plate armor begins to replace chain mail (*center*).

1307 Knights Templar disbanded by the French king Philip IV.

14th century Invention of gunpowder and cannon heralds end of castles and knights.

1415 Henry V's longbowmen defeat the French knights at the Battle of Agincourt.

1512 French cannons at the Battle of Ravenna prove that knights are no longer battle winners.

16th century Spanish Conquistadors reintroduce the horse to America.

1600 Native Americans first learn to train and ride horses.

1605–1615 Miguel de Cervantes Saavedra writes *Don Quixote*.

1620s Gustavus Adolphus integrates the cavalry into the rest of the army.

17th century First use of dragoons, riders armed with hand guns.

18th to 19th centuries Russian army uses Cossack (*bottom*) cavalry.

1854 Alfred Lord Tennyson writes *The Charge of the Light Brigade* following the Battle of Balaclava.

1914–1918 World War I sees the first aerial dogfights, and the invention of the tank.

1939 Polish lancers fight a losing battle against German tanks at the start of World War II.

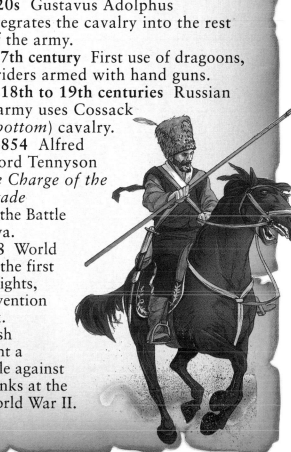

INDEX

Photo Credits (*Abbreviations: t – top, m – middle, b – bottom, r – right, l – left*).
Cover, 4-5, 7b, 10tl, 12-13, 14m, 18, 19t, 25, 26m, 28m, 29, 32t, 33, 37t & m, 39br, 40t & m, 43t & br – Mary Evans Picture Library; 6, 7t, 15, 16, 17, 21b, 31m, 32m, 36, 41, 44, 45tr & br – Frank Spooner Pictures; 8t, 21t & 28-29 – Ancient Art & Architecture Collection; 8b – Paramount Pictures (courtesy Kobal Collection); 9 – MGM (courtesy Kobal Collection); 11tr – 20th Century Fox (courtesy Kobal Collection); 14b & 31t & b – Stewart Ross; 19b & 27t & m – Ronald Grant Archive; 23 & 42-43 – Bridgeman Art Library; 27 – Columbia/Warner (courtesy Kobal Collection); 28t & bl & br – Roger Vlitos; 30 – Eye Ubiquitous; 35t – Hulton Deutsch; 35m – Warner Brothers (courtesy Kobal Collection); 43bl – Tom Donovan Military Pictures; 45ml – Lucas Films/20th Century Fox (courtesy Kobal Collection).